HEY, LiTTLE BUG!

POEMS FOR LiTTLE CREATURES

Poems by
JAMES CARTER

Illustrations by
MIQUE MORIUCHI

F

FRANCES LINCOLN
CHILDREN'S BOOKS

Contents

Welcome to creatures bugs and all welcome to readers big or small...

Welcome to *Hey, Little Bug!*

This book means a great deal to me because it was inspired by my two daughters when they were very young, and because the poems very much represent the world as seen through their eyes: 'Hey, look, Daddy, there's a caterpillar!' 'Daddy, this box is my home now.' 'Can I touch the moon now, Daddy?' I wouldn't have written any of these poems if it hadn't been for them allowing me the privilege of viewing the world afresh.

Many of the poems in *Hey, Little Bug!* I regularly perform at library events, book festivals and in Infant/Foundation classrooms all over the country. I have actions that I use to accompany the words as I find this helps to engage the young listener/ reader. Please feel free to make up your own actions! I do hope that you and your own little bugs have fun with these poems.

James Carter

Happy Poem

Happy as a rainbow
happy as a bee
happy as a dolphin
splashing in the sea

Happy as bare feet
running on the beach
happy as a sunflower
happy as a peach

Happy as a poppy
happy as a spoon
dripping with honey
happy as June

Happy as a banjo
plucking on a tune
happy as a Sunday
lazy afternoon

Happy as a memory
shared by two
happy as me...
when I'm with you!

Busy Bugs

Out in the garden
look down low
see all the busy bugs
come and go

Wriggly bugs
that can't keep still

Tiny bugs
that build a hill

Shiny bugs
that feed on leaves

Spotty bugs
that climb up trees

Out in the garden...

Noisy bugs
that live in grass

Bouncy bugs
that move so fast

Crawly bugs
that hide in sand

Tickly bugs
that like your hand!

Out in the garden…

11

Bug Hug

gimme a hug!   Hey,
      little   *gimme a hug!*
bug – how
do you hug –
or cuddle or kiss
gimme a hug!   your mum or sis –   *gimme a hug!*
with all those arms
and legs and things –
and wiggly bits and
wobbly wings? For
gimme a hug!   however hairy or   *gimme a hug!*
creepy or scary
even the ugliest
bug needs
a HUG!

12

Bed Bugs

We love to bite – oh yes, it's true
if you were a bug
then so would you!

When you're at play
we're starved all day
when you drop off
we have our scoff!

Life is good
and that's for sure
but hey, you humans

PLEASE
DON'T
SNORE!

Caterpillar

Caterpillar – in the sun
caterpillar – having fun
caterpillar – you're my chum!

Caterpillar – creep and crawl
caterpillar – up the wall
caterpillar – ten feet tall!

Caterpillar – way up high
caterpillar – in the sky
caterpillar…? **BUTTERFLY!**

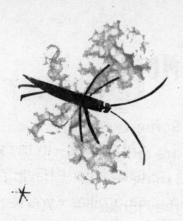

Butterflies

Those showy-offy butterflies
really aren't so very wise.

Who cares if they've got pretty wings?
Butterflies are snooty things!

Moths

Some say moths
are rather drab
I think
they look
really fab

And why
should insects
have to bother
dressing up
in fancy clobber?

One request
I have
is this:
may I
ask you
not to dis
– respect the moth
it's so unfair –
a moth's
got nothing
else to wear.

A Sticky Riddle

Wherever
I roam
I'm close
to home
and leave a
silver
trail.
In mist
or frost
I'm never
lost
because
I
am
a…?

Grasshopper

Grasshopper
fasthopper

zipping nipping
past hopper

high hopper
grasshopper

where's
  it
    gone?

Here it comes
again hopper

bouncing all
the way hopper

non-stopper
grasshopper

going

going

GONE!

The Spider and the Fly

Said the spider to the fly,
'You're a funny little guy –

and yet I find I love you so.'
'So set me free,' said Fly. 'Oh no!'

said Spider. 'Here is fine.
Let's relax and soon we'll dine.'

'Dine?' said Fly. 'There's no food here!'
Spider grinned. 'It's you, my dear.'

Bye Bye Ladybird

I'm spotty
I'm dotty
I'm lovely
and red

I live
in your garden
a leaf
is my bed

I'm tiny
I'm titchy
I've come to say
'Hi!'

But I'm
in a hurry
so I'll say
'Bye bye!'

Spider's Web

Spider's web
is spider's home
is spider's world
that spider's grown

Spider's web
is spider's skill
at spinning circles
in a wheel

Spider weaves
the sticky thread
and makes a giant
magic bed

A magic grid
that spider climbs
a magic net
for feeding times

If creature breaks
the magic frame
then spider builds it
back again

If breezes blow
bring flow and ebb
then spider clings
to spider's web

And spun with tender
loving care –
the greatest palace
anywhere

What Can It Be...?

A...

stripy-jumper
  flower-lover

happy-hummer
  must-be-summer

garden-grower
  come-and-goer

pollen-spreader
  swotter-dreader

black-and-yeller
  busy-fella

super-stinger
  honey-bringer

Pop outside
go and see
over there:
it's a...BEE!

Firefly

Dear firefly
do tell my why

you shine at night.
Do you store light –

a scoop of sun
inside your tum?

The Bear Came Down from the Mountain

The bear
    came
       down
          from
            the
               mountain
yawning the morning away

And scratching
  and sniffing
and stretching
  and itching
and fishing…
  for most of the day!

The bear went into the forest
hoping to find some tea

And stuffing
  and sticking
and picking
  and licking
the honey…
  he took from a tree!

                              mountain
                        the
                  up
            back
      went
The bear
yawning from having his fun

And hopping
  and skipping
and humming
  and singing
and happy…
  with food in his tum
with honey and fish
  in his tum… Y U M !

Bears Bears Bears!

Grizzly bears
honey bears
little titchy funny bears

Furry bears
huggy bears
  bears bears bears!

Black bears
brown bears
see them all around bears

Mummy Daddy
Baby bears
  bears bears bears!

Beige bears
white bears
hunting in the night bears
hiding from the light bears
creeping out of sight bears
giving you a fright bears
   bears bears bears!

Bears in the mountain
bears in the stream
bears in the deep wood
we've never been

Bears in the bedroom
little teddy bears
bears in the ice lands
   bears bears bears!

Bears in the starlight
snuggle up tight
bears in the winter
say **GOOD NIGHT!**

Snow Fox

Snow fox
go fox
out on her own

Snow fox
go fox
searching for home

Snow fox
go fox
on through the storm

Snow fox
go fox
somewhere warm

Snow fox
go fox
hungry and brave

Snow fox
go fox
find a cave

Snow fox
sleep fox
wait till dawn

Snow fox
rest fox
four cubs born

What Am I?

A...

sea-lover
> beach-hater

deep-diver
> wave-maker

great-gusher
> super-crusher

tail-flipper
> big-dipper

boat-tipper
> sea-sipper

> To make a splash
> I never fail.
> Have you guessed?
> I'm a... WHALE!

34

Dinosaurs...
Where Are They?

There's always more
to a dinosaur
than meets the eye.
They're ever so high,
as well as wide.
So how do they hide?

Disguised as mountains?
Or maybe trees?
Or under the seas?
And tell me now –
where've they gone?
They've been hiding
far too long!

Missing: DAISY

Anyone seen my D R A G O N ?
Scary, Scaly
Tall 'n Taily
Daisy the Dreadful Dragon.

She's got bad breath.
A temper true.
Eats old ladies. (Children too.)

She breathes out fire.
She puffs out smoke.
She'll singe your hair. She'll make you choke.

Anyone seen my D R A G O N ?...

She soars about.
She seeks out food.
Makes loud noises. (Mainly rude.)

Yes, she's grumpy.

Yes, she's smelly.

Big butt always blocks the telly.

Anyone seen my D R A G O N ?...

And she's beastly.

And a pest.

But I love her. (She's the best.)

Please send Daisy

back to me.

Treat her well. Or you'll be tea...

Anyone seen my D R A G O N ?...

Have You Seen My Cat?

She's got…

A thick black coat
with sticky-up fur
the tallest tail
the loudest purr

Ten white whiskers
four paddy paws
four white socks
and curly claws

Hang on –
is that her now?

Meowwww!

The What?

What moves clouds across the sky?
What makes waves rise up so high?
Clothes on lines – what blows them dry?

Autumn time – what spreads the seeds?
What tickles trees and scatters leaves?
What's often there, but no one sees?

What's over water, over land?
What can't be seen, but kicks up sand?
What pushes, pulls, without a hand?

the wind

 the wind

the wind

Seed

To way up high
from down below
the little seed
will grow and grow

And day by day
and hour by hour
the little seed
becomes a flower

The tiny shoot
so thin and green
will climb until
it can be seen

Into daylight
through the air
higher higher
nearly there

Grows until
the journey's done
then flower's happy
in the sun

Puddle Time

In Winter, Summer, Autumn, Spring
puddles really are the thing
to wash away the rainy blues
so put aside your walking shoes
they're no good for now you know –
find your wellies, off we go!

Puddles big and puddles small
puddles any size at all
at the park and down the lane
puddle time is here again!

Do a splish
do a splosh
let your wellies
have a wash!

Stomping stamping
in the rain
puddle time
is here again!

SPLISH SPLASH SPLOSH!

Babies in the bath do it
puddles on the path do it
grannies for a laugh do it

   Splish Splash Splosh!

Dirty welly boots do it
dainty little shoes do it
drippy doggies too do it

   Splish Splash Splosh!

Waterfalls and waves do it
giant killer whales do it
little fishes' tails do it

   Splish Splash Splosh!

Buses rushing past do it
rivers flowing fast do it
raindrops fall at last do it

   Splish Splash Splosh!

Swimmers in the pool do it
penguins in the zoo do it
dolphins in the blue do it

Splish Splash Splosh!

In the summer sun do it
do it as it's fun do it
come on everyone do it

Splish Splash Splosh!

Bubbles

Red bubble
yellow bubble
orange bubble blue

Pink bubble
purple bubble
rainbow bubble too

This bubble
big bubble
shiny and round

Float bubble
fly bubble
rise from the ground

Up bubble
up bubble
up so high

Go bubble
go bubble
gone –
bye bye!

It's Where?

It's where mermaids call their home
it's where pirates used to roam
it's where penguins have their tea
it's where people like to be

    It's deep it's damp it's big it's blue
    it's green it's grey it's turquoise too
    it's freezing cold and wild and yet
    it could be called the world-wide-wet

It's where baby clouds are made
it's where children love to bathe
it's where toddlers often wee –
to you and me it's called the...SEA!

Where Did We Go?

We bought a ticket to… Kalamazoo
we went by train
by boat, by plane
around the world
and back again
through night and day
through sun and rain
through mist and snow…

Then where did we go?

We bought a ticket to… Timbuktu
we went by train
by boat, by plane…

Then where did we go?

We bought a ticket to… Katmandu
we went by train
by boat, by plane…

Then where did we go?

We bought a ticket to…
[you choose some places!]
we went by train
by boat, by plane…

Then where did we go?

We bought a ticket to Kalamazoo
to Timbuktu
to Katmandu
to [your places!]

we went by train
by boat, by plane
around the world
and back again
through night and day
through sun and rain
through mist and snow

Then where did we go?

Home
    sweet
        home!

Kalamazoo

Train, Train

Train, train,
travelling, travelling,
where are you going to?
Can I come too?
Train, train,
travelling, travelling,
where have you been to?
What have you seen?

I'm –
off to the city and
off to the sea and
off to the valley and
back home for tea.

Train, train…

Then –
into the tunnel and
under the bridge
down to the river and
over the ridge.

Train, train…

I'm picking up passengers,
picking up mail,
picking up speed,
I follow the rail.

Train, train…

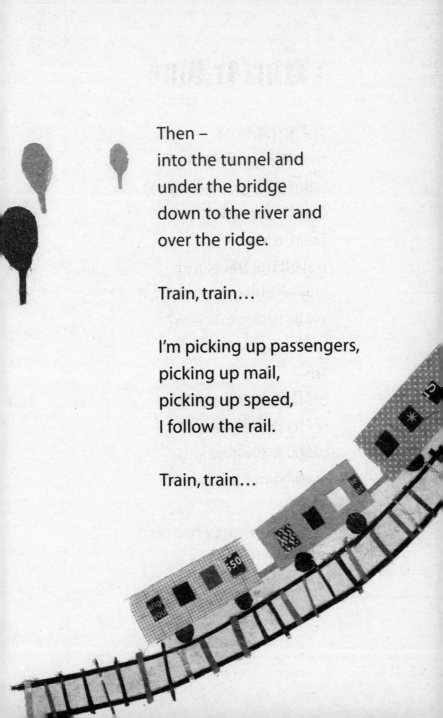

Tractor Blue

The farmer's
in his tractor
his dog
is by his side

The tractor
is all shiny blue
the wheels
are high and wide

The farmer waves
the old dog barks
the tractor
rolls along

And now they're going
harvesting
to bring in
all the corn!

Little Boat

Little boat
it makes me sad
to think that
you will never have

the chance to sail
upon the sea
and yet I'm glad
you're here with me

and that you'll float
between my knees
in these bubbly
soapy seas
so after all…
I think I'm pleased!

Pirate Pete

Pirate Pete
had a ship on the sea
had a fish for his tea
had a peg for a knee

    and a tiny little parrot called... Polly

Pirate Pete
had a book with a map
had a skull on his cap
had a cat on his lap

    and another little parrot called... Dolly

Pirate Pete
had a trunk full of treasure
had a belt made of leather
had a cap with a feather

    and another little parrot called... Jolly

Pirate Pete
had a patch on his eye
had a flag he would fly
had a plank way up high

and another little parrot called... Molly

So Pirate Pete
and the parrots four
they sailed the world
from shore to shore –
collecting gold
and gifts galore.
And that's their tale...
there is no more!

Shell

I found this shell
in a rockpool

I dipped my hand
in the water

I dried the shell
and I took it home

I keep it safe
under my pillow

I hold the shell
and shut my eyes

I watch the waves
crash on the beach

I feel the water
tickle my toes

I hear the sea
deep in my dreams

I found this shell
in a rockpool

Circle Poem

I want to be a circle

A
curly-wurly
roly-round

A bounce me up
and off the ground

A circle – like a spinning top
a circle – like a ticking clock
a circle – like a moon so tall
a circle – like a bouncy ball

I want to be a circle

A circle – like a plastic hoop
a circle – like a loop-the-loop
a circle – like a whizzing wheel
a circle – like a pizza meal

I
want to be
I want to be
I want to be
A CIRCLE
!

Marble

Little marble
in my hand
full of wonder
magic – and

bring me luck
in all I do
and in return
I'll cherish you

Ticklish?

You can tickle
my feet
you can tickle
my toes
you can tickle
just a little
on the tip
of my nose

With a finger
    or a feather
        you can tickle me
            however…

But I won't
    even snigger…
        OH NO!

Hands

Hands are for waving
hello or goodbye

Hands are for wiping
the tears that you cry

Hands are for stretching
or reaching up tall

Hands are for throwing
or catching a ball

Hands are for clapping
in time to the beat

Hands are for cooking
the food that we eat

Hands are for brushing
your teeth and your hair

Hands are for drawing
or hands are for prayer

Hands are for working
and hands are for play

Hands are for helping
you get through each day

Listen To The Rhythm

Listen to the rhythm
when hands go
CLAP!

Listen to the rhythm
when feet go
TAP!

Listen to the rhythm
when rain goes
SPLASH!

Listen to the rhythm
when cymbals
CRASH!

Listen to the rhythm
when clocks go
TICK!

Listen to the rhythm
when taps go
DRIP!

Listen to the rhythm
when bells go
CLANG!

Listen to the rhythm
when drums go
BANG!

Listen to the rhythm
go :

      CLAP CLAP CLAP!

      TAP TAP TAP!

      CRASH CRASH CRASH!

      SPLASH SPLASH SPLASH!

      TICK TICK TICK!

      DRIP DRIP DRIP!

      CLANG CLANG CLANG!

      BANG BANG BANG!

Listen to the rhythm
of **E V E R Y T H I N G !**

Little But LOUD

Little
birdie cutie
thing – it's
so lovely
when
you
sing

tweetie tweetie cheep cheep cheep

but
turn
it
down –
I need
to sleep!

Sounds Nice

Millie plays the tambourine
up and down and in between
taps it lightly rolls it round
shakes it wildly on the ground
    shaking once
    shaking twice
Millie makes it sound so nice

Oscar plays the saxophone
in a band and on his own
Oscar makes a super sound
honking tooting soft or loud
    honking once
    honking twice
Oscar makes it sound so nice

Erin plays the violin
holds it tight beneath her chin
swirling round now watch her go
striking swiftly with her bow
    bowing once
    bowing twice
Erin makes it sound so nice

Dylan plays the double bass
takes it all around the place
see him swing it round and round
fingers plucking up and down
    plucking once
    plucking twice
Dylan makes it sound so nice

Shaking once
    honking twice
bowing plucking
    sounds so nice!

Cardboard Box

I've got this box
and it's all mine
I pop in there
from time to time

It's like a den
or hide-away
a secret place
that's out the way

It's where I go
to be alone
it's safe in there
a tiny home

My cardboard box?
I love it lots!

Naughty Step

A there now – are
you better? step.
A tear might wet
the carpet step.
A wait until I
tell you step.
A stop and think
about it step.
A stay there till
you're sorry step.
The bottom step
is the naughty step.

My Bedroom

My bedroom
My best room
My oh-what-a-mess room

My day room
My play room
My out-of-the-way room

My come-take-a-look room
My read-me-a-book room

My turn-out-the-light room
my snuggle-up-tight room

My 'Mum-I-can't-sleep' room
my hide-and-my-seek room

My go-have-a-rest room
my snug-as-a-nest room

My bounce-on-the-bed room
my lovely-old-ted room

My best room?
My bedroom!

The Key

This is the key
this is the door
this is the rug
down on the floor

This is our photo
up on the wall
this is the phone
out in the hall

This is the table
these are the chairs
see over here
these are the stairs

This is the landing
this is the light
this is my room
I sleep here at night

This is my family
this is me
this is my home
this is the key

First Day

First day
feeling new
don't know what
to say or do

First day
feeling funny
by the door
cling to Mummy

First day
feeling shy
really trying
not to cry

First day
feeling wrong
morning seems
so very long

First day
feeling strange
don't know
anybody's name

First day
on the mat
dress up in
a wizard's hat

First day
play outside
find a bike
and have a ride

First day
write my name
have a drink
and play a game

First day
carpet time:
read a book
and say a rhyme

First day
out the gate
back tomorrow –
can't wait!

Show and Tell

Amber showed a little shell
Bella told us how she fell
Carla went to see her nan
Daniel went to see West Ham
Ella did a ballet dance
Faron's daddy went to France
Georgia talked about her aunty
Hannah's going to have a party
Ian brought his football cards
Joey showed his model cars
Kieran told us he'd been naughty
Lauren counted up to forty
Maddie sang her favourite song
Noah's baby won't be long
Ollie went to Daniel's home
Paris had an ice-cream cone
Quentin showed a paper swan
Rohan's brother's nearly one
Sarah made a frog with clay

Tina's nana came to stay
Usha's learning how to swim
Vinny brought some acorns in
Winston laughed and told a joke
MaX put on his wizard's cloak
Yasmine said a funny rhyme
Zoe said she'd show next time

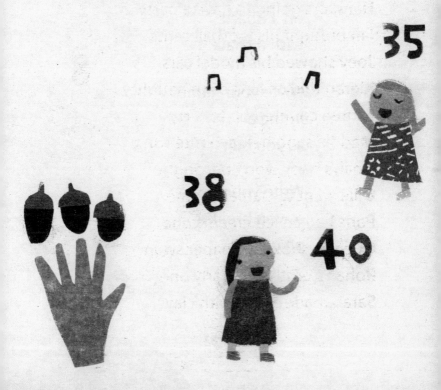

Write Your Name

Write your name
with a stick
in the sand

Write your name
in the snow
with your hand

Write your name
on a board
with a chalk

Write your name
in the air
as you talk

Write your name
as you breathe
on glass

Write your name
with your friends
in class

Write your name
all curly
and small

Write your name
all pointy
and tall

Write your name
in the dark
at night

Write your name
in the sky
with a kite

Write your name
whatever you do –
write your name
to celebrate
        YOU!

Crayon Poem

With these **crayons**
I could draw…

A scary
purple dinosaur.

An **orange** mouse
with **yellow** cheese.

A big **brown** dog
with big **black** fleas.

A tall **blue** house
with a small **green** door
and four **white** windows.

Something more?

Silver raindrops.
Golden sun.

Then a...**R A I N B O W**

sounds like fun!

With these crayons
I could draw
                    so
                            much
                                    more!

Dream Pie

(a recipe for sleepy-heads)

Take…

The rubbing of eyes
the climbing of stairs
the brushing of teeth
the cuddling of bears

The reading of books
the kissing of Mum
the counting of sheep
and now it is done…

In only a while
you will be yawning
next thing you'll know
it will be morning!

Excuses Excuses

I'm sitting here
at the top of the stairs
wondering what
I should say:

I can't get to sleep?

I feel a bit poorly?

I maybe heard a mouse?

The dark's too dark?

My brain keeps thinking?

Now which one will get me
a biscuit and a milk
and a little bit
of grown-up telly?

One Eye Open

I'm keeping one eye open
just in case I see
the fairy come and take my tooth
and leave me 50p

Little Dreamer

Climb into bed now
snuggle up tight
deep in the duvet
warm in the night

Go little dreamer
safe and slow
off to the world
where memories grow

Bed is a boat
to sail you away
and bring you back
to a brand new day.

James Carter is a prize-winning poet,
guitarist and educational writer.
He travels all over the UK to give lively
poetry performances, workshops,
gifted and talented days and INSET sessions.
Hey, Little Bug! is his first book for
Frances Lincoln.
James lives in Wallingford with his wife,
2 daughters, 3 cats and 4 guitars.

www.jamescarterpoet@btinternet.com

978-1-84780-167-8 • PB • £5.99

With wordplay and riddles, and poems that will make
you laugh, tell you stories and make you think, this is
a brilliant debut from an exciting new poet.

"A box of delights" – *Carol Ann Duffy*

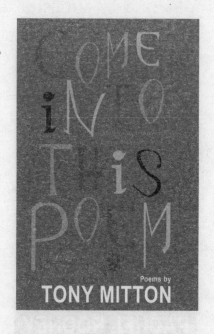

Poems by
TONY MITTON

978-1-84780-169-2 • PB • £5.99

From spooky legends to dreamy poems, teasers
and rhymes, expect the unexpected. A poetry adventure
waiting to happen!

"A poet with a powerful feeling for story
and language" – *Carousel*